BEYOND THE WORDS

How Good Men Connect with Women

BY LOGAN HART

First Edition — November 2025

Logan Hart Publishing LLC — Springfield, Illinois

ISBN 979-8-218-84657-2

Printed and Published in the United States of America

DEDICATION

To the good men who refuse to believe that good men finish last. To those who love deeply, listen intentionally, and lead with grace.

To every man learning to love beyond his words — this book is for you.

For the ones who've been misunderstood for their kindness, taken for granted for their steadiness, or doubted because they chose peace over pride — may this remind you that goodness is not weakness.

It is strength under control, faith under pressure, and love that endures.

Author's Preface

WHAT THIS BOOK IS (AND ISN'T)

This book isn't written to help men get women — it's written to help good men understand them.

It's not a manual for manipulation or a playbook for control. It's a compass for communication — a way to navigate love when logic runs out and emotion takes the wheel.

There are enough voices out there teaching men how to perform — how to say the right thing, wear the right look, or act the right part. But this isn't that kind of message. Love isn't a strategy. It's a stewardship. It's how a man honors what he's been given without demanding what he thinks he deserves.

If you came here looking for tricks, you'll be disappointed. But if you came here looking for truth — about yourself, about the woman you love, and about what it means to love like a man of faith — then this book will speak to you.

Love has no guarantees. There's no formula that promises affection or assures forever. But there is a way to love that leaves peace in your heart — knowing you did your part with honesty, patience, and respect.

Some people say, "Find a fool, bump their head." That's the mindset of a world that confuses goodness with gullibility. Being a good man doesn't mean being naive — it means being grounded. It means having the wisdom to recognize manipulation and the courage to walk away from it, even when your heart wants to stay.

Good doesn't mean easy. Good means steady. It means standing firm in a world that celebrates chaos and calls it passion. It means staying gentle when you could be harsh, humble when you could be proud, faithful when you could be free.

This book was written to restore that meaning — to make "good" mean strong again. Strong enough to lead with love. Strong enough to forgive without being foolish. Strong enough to walk away without bitterness.

If that's the kind of man you're trying to be, this book was written with you in mind.

"Let all that you do be done in love." — 1 Corinthians 16:14

— Logan Hart

CONTENTS

INTRODUCTION

There's a quiet kind of pain that good men carry — the kind that comes from trying to love right but never feeling fully understood. It's the ache of a heart that gives, not to be noticed, but because it's how you were raised — to protect, to provide, to persevere.

Most of us learned early how to fix things, but not how to feel through them. We were taught to work, to endure, to stand tall when the world leaned heavy — but rarely to speak tenderness, to express hurt, or to say, "I need you too."

Yet every man who's ever truly loved knows this truth: strength alone doesn't sustain love — understanding does.

This book isn't about changing who you are. It's about refining how you love. It's for the men who believe that faith still matters, that communication still heals, and that effort still counts.

Each chapter invites you to reflect, to pray, and to grow — not through guilt, but through grace. You'll find real stories, practical guidance, and spiritual reminders that show how a man can remain both strong and soft — firm in principle, but open in heart.

This isn't a "how to win her back" book. It's a "how to love with wisdom" book. Because loving a woman — truly loving her — means learning her rhythms, respecting her emotions, and leading with humility.

It's written in a man's rhythm but with a woman's heart in mind. It's for every man who wants to listen beyond the words, discern what she's really saying, and build the kind of emotional safety that keeps love alive.

Whether you're in a new relationship, rebuilding one, or recovering from one that broke you, let this book remind you of something simple and sacred:

Love isn't lost. It's learned.

"And now these three remain: faith, hope, and love. But the greatest of these is love."

— 1 Corinthians 13:13

SPECIAL THANKS

To Tee, the one who inspired these pages — your presence and your absence both taught me what connection really means. You reminded me that love is not measured by how close two people stand, but by how much faith they keep when miles stand between them.

And to every reader walking through love, loss, or rediscovery — you are not alone. May this book meet you where you are, and lift you to where grace can do its work

Chapter

1

WHEN HER WORLD SHAKES

"His fiance had just lost her uncle. The family was gathering, emotions were high, and then came more difficult news — her daughter had called to say that her own son was going through serious problems. The weight of it all hit her hard. He wanted to be there for her, but distance made that impossible. So instead, he sent up prayers — for her, for her daughter, and for her grandson. He lifted them all to God, trusting that his love and faith would reach them where his presence could not. And in that moment, he realized — love doesn't always fix; sometimes it simply stands, even from afar."

When a woman is hurting, a man's first instinct is to do something — to repair, protect, explain, or reason through it. But emotional pain can't always be solved with logic or action.

Sometimes the best thing you can offer isn't an answer, it's presence — even if that presence has to be spiritual, not physical.

You don't have to know all the right words. You just have to keep her covered in prayer, steady in faith, and consistent in your care.

"Rejoice with those who rejoice; mourn with those who mourn." — Romans 12:15

Expanded Reflection — The Power of Silent Strength

There's a moment every good man faces — the moment when love won't let him fix everything. It's humbling, even painful, because we're wired to fix.

We want to stop the pain, solve the problem, and close the distance.

But what women remember most isn't what we do — it's how we show up.

It's the quiet "I'm here" text when words won't come easily. It's the calm tone that steadies her storm. It's being dependable in a world that's constantly changing. Silent strength doesn't make headlines, but it moves hearts. Every time you choose patience over panic, you teach her that she's safe — not because you're perfect, but because you're present. And when she knows she's safe with you, even silence becomes sacred.

Faith in Action — When You Can't Be There

Sometimes God allows distance to teach us how to love without control. You might not be able to hold her, but you can still hold her up in prayer.

You might not be able to fix the situation, but you can remain a steady reminder that she's not alone.

Prayer travels where your hands cannot. Faith sustains when words fall short. Patience becomes a language of its own. When you surrender your need to fix, you make room for God to move. And that's when love matures — when you're powerless to change, but strong enough to stay.

Practical Example — When Distance Tests Devotion

Maybe you've been there — watching someone you love go through something heavy while you're miles away. You call, you text, you wait. The helplessness feels like failure. But it isn't.

Your love isn't less real just because it's quiet. Sometimes love is proven through patience — the kind that stays when the spotlight fades, the kind that still checks in long after others have stopped asking how she's doing.

When you choose to love like that, you're building something eternal — not emotional convenience, but spiritual commitment.

Checklist — When Her World Shakes

1. Pray first — for her peace and your patience.

2. Respond, don't rescue — she may need comfort more than correction.

3. Communicate safety — say, "I'm here when you're ready to talk."

4. Guard against frustration — her silence isn't rejection; it's processing.

5. Stay faithful in the wait — love's strength is measured by its endurance.

6. Keep perspective — storms reveal foundations; don't take them personally.

7. Be consistent — even small gestures matter more during crisis.

Expanded Reflection — When Faith Holds the Line

Real love is spiritual before it's emotional. When you cover her in prayer instead of pressure, you become a partner in God's healing process.

Sometimes the best way to show love is to stay the course.

Don't run because she withdraws. Don't demand because she's distant. Stand firm in peace. Let your steadiness become her shelter.

You may not see immediate results, but love planted in patience always blooms in time.

Closing Reflection — Still Standing

Good men aren't always the loudest; sometimes they're the ones holding the line when everything else falls apart.

You don't need to fix her to love her well.

You just need to stay grounded in faith when her foundation shakes.

When you remain steady through the storm, you prove that love doesn't have to shout to be strong — it just has to stand.

Chapter

2

RECOGNIZING HER
NEEDS AND LOVE LANGUAGES

"When a man learns the language of her heart, he's not just speaking — he's connecting."

Every woman feels love differently.

Some hear it through words. Others feel it through time, touch, service, or thoughtful gestures.

A man can say "I love you" every day and still miss her completely if he's not saying it in the language her heart understands.

It's easy to assume love is universal, but love is personal.

You can't love her well if you're loving her only in the way you prefer.

You love well when you study her — when you notice what lights her up, what soothes her, what makes her feel seen.

Expanded Reflection — Her Language Is Her Lifeline

Every woman has a rhythm — a way her heart feels safe and known.

When you love her in her language, you're saying, "I see you in ways the world overlooks." That's not weakness; that's wisdom.

Learning her love language isn't a chore; it's worship.

It's a daily choice to prioritize connection over convenience. It's not about performing; it's about paying attention.

When you stop guessing and start observing, you discover that love is less about the big moments and more about the little consistencies — the good-morning text, the extra hug when she's quiet, the small act of service that reminds her she's worth the effort.

The Moment He Learned Her Language

He worked long hours, fixed things around the house, paid every bill on time. Yet she still felt distant. One night she whispered, "I just wish you'd sit with me — not to talk, just to be here." It hit him. He'd been speaking Acts of Service, but her language was Quality Time. He hadn't been neglectful — just untranslated.

The next evening, he put the tools down early. No screens, no distractions. Just presence. It didn't take long before she relaxed again — not because he did something new, but because he finally did what spoke to her.

That one quiet evening taught him more about love than any grand gesture ever had.

Faith Insight — Love as Stewardship

"Husbands, love your wives, just as Christ loved the church and gave Himself up for her." — Ephesians 5:25

Love that reflects God is self-sacrificing, not self-serving. It listens before it leads.

It asks, "How can I honor her heart today?" instead of, "What am I getting out of this?" When you love her this way, you're not losing power — you're gaining purpose.

Everyday Examples — How She Hears Love

- Words of Affirmation : "I'm proud of you. You make this house a home."

- Quality Time: Put down the phone. Give her your full attention.

- Acts of Service: Handle a task before she has to ask.

- Physical Touch: A gentle hand on her shoulder when she's anxious.

- Gifts: Something thoughtful that says, "I was thinking of you."

The goal isn't to pick just one — it's to learn her rhythm and speak it fluently enough that she feels secure, even on the days you fall short.

Expanded Reflection — When Love Is Lost in Translation

So many arguments in relationships aren't about what's being said — they're about what's not being heard. A woman who values words may feel unloved if she only sees actions.

A woman who values presence may feel lonely even while sitting beside you if your attention is somewhere else.

You can be faithful but disconnected. You can be loyal but unavailable.

When you finally grasp that her needs are not demands — they're her language — you begin to love her with intention, not assumption.

Checklist — Recognizing and Responding to Her Needs

1. Study, don't assume. Pay attention to what brings her peace, not just smiles.

2. Be flexible. Her language can shift during stress or seasons.

3. Give without keeping score. Real love is not a transaction.

4. Validate emotion. You don't have to agree — just acknowledge.

5. Pray for understanding. Ask God to reveal what words cannot.

6. Listen to feedback without defense. Love matures when it adjusts.

Faith Reflection — When God Translates Love

Every time you ask God to show you how to love her better, you invite Him into your relationship. He knows her heart better than you ever will. Let Him teach you. Let patience become your vocabulary and kindness your tone.

Love that is learned through prayer always outlasts love that is lived through pride.

Closing Reflection — The Good Man Learns Her Language

A good man doesn't need to be fluent in everything — just fluent in her. He studies affection, not attention. He listens for cues instead of waiting for complaints. He shows love in the ways she can feel it, not just see it. When you learn her language, love stops being confusing — it becomes communion.

Chapter

3

LISTEN, LISTEN, LISTEN — AND HEAR HER

"When a woman speaks, she's not always asking for answers. Sometimes she just needs to know that her heart has a safe place to land." Most men want to solve things. We hear a problem, and our mind starts building solutions before she finishes her sentence. But for her, communication isn't always about fixing — it's about feeling safe enough to share.

To a woman, being heard is being loved. When she opens up, she's not just venting; she's handing you the map to her emotional world. What you do with it determines whether she keeps sharing or starts shutting down.

Listening isn't silence. It's presence. It's eye contact, empathy, and patience. It's choosing not to interrupt, not to defend, not to debate — just to understand.

Expanded Reflection — Hearing the Heart Behind the Words

A man who listens only for information will miss the message every time. But a man who listens for emotion will hear what most men never notice.

Sometimes what she's really saying is hidden behind what she says. "I'm fine" might mean, "I feel disconnected."

"I don't want to talk right now" might mean, "I don't feel safe talking yet." Listening is how you translate those moments without judgment.

You don't have to fix every feeling — just hold space for it. Your stillness gives her security. Your patience gives her peace. She'll remember your calm more than your conclusions.

Faith Insight — Listening as a Spiritual Discipline

"Everyone should be quick to listen, slow to speak, and slow to become angry." — James 1:19

God listens before He corrects. He doesn't rush to reply; He lets our hearts unfold.

When you take that same posture in your relationship, you're reflecting divine patience. Listening isn't passive — it's powerful. It's how you love a woman the way Christ loves His people: fully, attentively, and without haste. Listening well is an act of worship — it honors both her heart and God's design for connection.

Everyday Example — When He Learned to Pause

He used to interrupt mid-sentence, trying to fix everything. She'd go quiet, exhausted from explaining the same things. One night she said softly, "I just wanted you to listen."

The next time, he didn't speak. He just nodded, leaned in, and said, "That sounds really hard." Her shoulders dropped. Her eyes softened. She exhaled. She didn't need his advice — she needed his attention.

And for the first time, she felt safe being fully herself again.

Expanded Reflection — When Listening Heals What Words Can't

There's a kind of love that doesn't need to talk — it just knows how to be still together. That's what most women are craving: not a man who always has an answer, but one who can be a safe silence.

When you listen like that, arguments fade faster, emotions settle quicker, and connection lasts longer. You stop trying to win and start trying to understand. And that's where love grows roots.

Listening builds safety — and safety is what keeps love standing when emotion wears thin.

Practical Guidance — Listening That Builds Safety

1. Be fully present. No phone, no distractions — she can feel divided attention.

2. Reflect, don't react. Say, "I hear you," or "That makes sense."

3. Listen for emotion, not just content. Hear the heart beneath the words.

4. Ask gentle follow-ups. "What do you need from me right now?"

5. Keep the space soft. Lower your voice, even when tension rises.

6. End with reassurance. A simple "We'll get through this" can be enough.

Checklist — Listening That Strengthens Connection

- Don't correct her feelings — acknowledge them.

- Mirror what she says to show understanding.

- Avoid phrases like "You always…" or "You never…"

- Choose the right timing — don't discuss heavy things when emotions are raw.

- End with prayer or reassurance, not pressure.

Faith Reflection — God Hears Before He Heals

Sometimes the most Christlike thing a man can do is simply listen.

You're not losing authority by listening — you're gaining trust. You're showing her that her thoughts have value, her emotions have space, and her voice has a place beside yours.

That's what partnership sounds like in action. Love that listens lasts longer than love that lectures.

Closing Thought — Love That Hears First

You can't argue a woman into feeling safe — you earn it by listening long enough for her to exhale. When you learn to hear her heart, not just her words, you unlock a level of connection that logic can't reach.

A good man doesn't just listen to respond.

He listens to understand — and in doing so, he teaches her that her soul has a home in his peace.

Chapter

4

BUILDING
TRUST AND CONSISTENCY

"She doesn't need perfection. She needs to know she can count on you — not just when things are good, but when life gets messy."

Trust doesn't happen in the big moments; it's built in the quiet ones. It grows in the pattern of your tone, your timing, and your truth.

It's proven not in what you say once, but in what you repeat faithfully.

A woman doesn't need a perfect man — she needs a consistent one. When she can predict your peace, she'll start to relax in your presence.

When she knows your words match your actions, she'll begin to open her heart without fear of regret.

Consistency turns affection into safety; reliability builds emotional shelter. Trust isn't built in a day — it's built daily.

Expanded Reflection — The Quiet Proof of Love

In the beginning, most men try hard to impress.

They show effort, make plans, send texts, and speak sweetly.

But after comfort sets in, consistency is often the first thing to fade.

That's where real love begins — after the novelty wears off and the discipline starts.

When your tone stays gentle, when your follow-through stays steady, when your heart stays kind even when she's stressed — that's what she remembers.

It's not the flowers; it's the follow-up.

It's not the grand gesture; it's the daily grace. It's not the apology; it's the adjustment.

Love doesn't need a speech — it needs repetition.

The quiet man who shows up predictably will always outlast the charming man who shows up occasionally.

Faith Insight — How God Defines Trust

"Whoever is faithful in little will also be faithful in much." — Luke 16:10

God doesn't test trust through success — He tests it through small assignments. He watches how we treat what's ordinary before He entrusts us with what's sacred. The same is true in love.

If she can trust you with her daily peace, she'll trust you with her deepest pain. Faithfulness in small things turns relationships into sanctuaries.

Everyday Example — When Consistency Spoke Louder Than Apologies

She said, "I don't need another sorry. I just need to see the change." So he stopped promising and started showing. He began texting when he said he would. He showed up on time. He prayed with her before bed.

After a while, she didn't need reassurance — she could see it.

Her guard fell not because of his words, but because of his rhythm. That's how consistency heals what apologies can't.

Expanded Reflection — When Trust Has Been Broken

When trust breaks, love doesn't die — but it becomes fragile. It flinches. It hesitates. It questions even kindness.

If that's where you are, understand this: rebuilding trust isn't about convincing her with promises; it's about calming her with proof.

You can't rush her healing. You can only reinforce it with reliability.

Every day that you stay consistent, her doubt loses strength.

Every day you choose peace over defensiveness, her heart feels safer.

You're not proving yourself to her — you're proving to both of you that faith can rebuild what fear tried to destroy.

Practical Framework — 7-Day Trust Reset Plan

1. Admit what broke the pattern. Own your part without excuses.

2. Ask what she needs to feel safe. Listen fully — don't defend.

3. Stay reachable. No vanishing acts; consistency requires accessibility.

4. Keep your word in small things. The little promises repair the big ones.

5. Let time prove your intent. Don't rush her healing; earn it.

6. Pray for humility. Pride delays progress.

7. End each day with gratitude. Thank her — and thank God — for another chance to build better.

Checklist — Building and Sustaining Trust

- Be predictable in peace.

- Keep your word short and steady.

- Admit fault quickly.

- Let time speak for you.

- Pray for strength, not control.

- Never use silence as punishment.

- Match consistency with compassion.

Faith Reflection — When Trust Mirrors God's Nature

Trust is love's echo of God's character. When you are steady, you reflect Him. When you keep showing up, even after mistakes, you show her that faithfulness still exists.

Consistency doesn't mean perfection — it means dependability.

And in a world that values charm over character, that kind of love stands out like light in the dark.

Closing Thought — The Weight of Steadiness

She doesn't need you to be amazing — she needs you to be available.

She doesn't need fireworks — she needs follow-through. She doesn't need perfection — she needs peace.

When you give her that, she'll stop wondering if she can trust you, because your consistency will answer that question for her every day.

Chapter

5

WHEN LOVE FEELS DISTANT

"He could feel her drifting — shorter texts, slower responses, quieter calls." Emotional distance rarely starts with an argument. It begins in the small spaces — fewer words, shorter hugs, less laughter. A good man feels it before he can explain it. Something shifts, something cools, and he starts wondering, What did I do?

When love starts to feel distant, panic wants to take over. You want to call more, explain more, fix more. But often, that only widens the gap.

Don't chase panic — pause and pray. Distance doesn't always mean disconnection; sometimes it means she's overwhelmed, processing, or simply protecting her peace. Your calm presence can do more healing than your constant questioning ever could.

Expanded Reflection — The Slow Fade of Connection

Relationships rarely crumble overnight. They fade quietly when gratitude turns into assumption and grace gives way to frustration. The laughter becomes shorter. The texts become routine. The warmth becomes obligation.

But here's what most people forget — distance isn't always death. Sometimes it's a warning light, not an ending. It's love saying, "We need maintenance."

If you can stay calm when emotion withdraws, you give love a chance to breathe again. Panic closes hearts. Patience reopens them.

When she feels you stop chasing and start steadying, she can find her way back without feeling cornered.

Faith Insight — Love That Endures the Quiet Season

"Be still, and know that I am God." — Psalm 46:10

Stillness is a spiritual posture. It's how we remind ourselves that we're not in control — God is. Sometimes the season of silence isn't punishment; it's preparation. God could be teaching both of you how to love without control, how to communicate without noise, and how to trust without constant reassurance. Stillness isn't weakness — it's wisdom. It's saying, "I don't have to chase what's meant for me."

Everyday Example — When Distance Wasn't the End

He noticed her pulling back. Calls were shorter, messages colder.

Instead of arguing or accusing, he started thanking her again — for her time, her effort, her spirit. It wasn't manipulation. It was gratitude.

And gratitude has power. Because love that feels unseen often just needs acknowledgment. A few weeks later, her warmth returned. Not because he pressured her, but because his peace reminded her why she loved him in the first place.

Expanded Reflection — The Discipline of Peace

When you feel her slipping away, you have two choices: react from fear or respond from faith. Fear will make you chase, overthink, and demand clarity before its time.

Faith will keep you steady, humble, and grounded in purpose. If love is drifting, focus on what you can control — your spirit. Don't let insecurity rewrite your story. Distance may be temporary; damage from desperation can be permanent.

Sometimes the best thing you can do is to keep showing kindness even when she doesn't respond the same way. That's not weakness — that's maturity.

Practical Framework — Bridging Silence with Softness

1. Acknowledge the shift. Don't pretend you don't feel it; approach it gently.

2. Lead with calm, not concern. Panic pushes; peace invites.

3. Rebuild small rituals of warmth. A kind word, a check-in, a prayer — little gestures remind her of safety.

4. Invite her thoughts without defense. Let her talk without fear of correction.

5. Pray for discernment. Ask God if this distance is for reflection or redirection.

6. Stay anchored. Don't let emotional storms pull you out of your character.

Checklist — When Love Feels Distant

- Don't assume the worst.

- Notice before you nag.

- Reconnect spiritually — pray for her, not about her.

- Invest without overextending.

- Be patient — love takes time to rewarm.

- Let time test truth.

- Keep gratitude louder than fear.

Faith Reflection — When God Uses Distance for Development

Sometimes God uses space to stretch both hearts. He allows distance so that dependence shifts — from each other to Him. It's not rejection; it's refinement.

If you can stay patient in this phase, you'll find that what feels like silence is actually the sound of growth happening beneath the surface. Faith doesn't beg to be seen — it believes quietly.

Closing Thought — Still Water Finds Its Depth

Don't chase her shadow — build your light. If she's meant to be part of your story, she'll find her way back to the warmth you kept alive. And if she doesn't, you'll still be standing in peace, because you loved with patience and led with grace. Love that rests in faith never really loses. It just learns how to last.

Chapter

6

IT TAKES TWO

"She wanted him to try harder; he wanted her to appreciate what he'd already done." Relationships don't thrive on one person's strength — they survive on two hearts working in rhythm. One-sided love eventually feels like carrying a heavy table alone: you can lift it for a while, but not forever.

Partnership is about balance — not equal in every moment, but equal in effort. It's about learning that both people must pour, both must pray, and both must protect what's being built.

A good man gives, but he can't carry love alone.

When both are trying — even imperfectly — the relationship becomes a team instead of a test.

Expanded Reflection — When Partnership Feels Uneven

Every couple faces moments when one person is giving more. Sometimes she's weary. Sometimes you are. That's normal.

But when one person always does the reaching, the initiating, the fixing — love starts to turn into labor. And the weight of that imbalance slowly kills connection.

Healthy love breathes when both people contribute to its oxygen — effort, respect, communication, and care. It's not about keeping score; it's about keeping faith.

You can't demand balance, but you can model it.

When you give with grace, you invite reciprocity instead of resentment. Real love doesn't need a scoreboard — it just needs shared sincerity.

Faith Insight — Unity as a Sacred Assignment

"Two are better than one, because they have a good return for their labor." — Ecclesiastes 4:9

God designed partnership to multiply strength, not drain it.

When both people honor the relationship with effort and humility, even hardships become opportunities for growth. Unity isn't about agreeing on everything — it's about fighting for the same thing: peace, purpose, and presence.

When you pray together, storms sound softer. When you listen together, pride loses power. And when you heal together, love becomes holy.

Everyday Example — Counseling That Worked

They were stuck — two good people on opposite ends of misunderstanding. She said, "You don't make me feel special anymore."

He said, "You don't appreciate what I do."

The counselor told them, "You're both right — and both missing each other." So they started ending each night with one simple ritual:

Each person said one sentence beginning with, "I'm thankful for…"

It felt awkward at first. But after a few weeks, their tone softened, and their laughter returned. They didn't fix everything — they simply remembered gratitude. Sometimes love doesn't need a restart — just a reminder.

Expanded Reflection — The 80/20 → 100 Principle

There will be seasons where one person can only give 80%. Maybe stress, grief, or exhaustion has drained them. That's when the other covers the difference, temporarily — not permanently.

The problem comes when 80% becomes the new normal. Love isn't sustainable when only one person keeps showing up.

The 80/20 → 100 principle means this:

When she's weak, you carry her with grace. When you're tired, she carries you with prayer. But both must still reach for the same 100 — the same shared goal of love that's reciprocal, respectful, and rooted in faith.

Practical Framework — Rebuilding as a Team

1. Check your tone before your point. Peace creates space for truth.

2. Invite her input instead of defending. Listening is leading.

3. Share spiritual leadership. Pray together, even when frustrated.

4. Practice the one-day rule. Don't make major decisions while angry.

5. Celebrate small wins out loud. Gratitude heals faster than criticism.

6. Don't weaponize effort. If you're doing it to get credit, it's not love — it's leverage.

Checklist — Practicing Partnership

- Equal ownership, not equal perfection.

- Shared responsibility for peace.

- Encourage growth, not guilt.

- Seek guidance early — don't wait until resentment grows.

- Pray daily for unity and understanding.

- Replace "me vs. you" with "us vs. the problem."

Faith Reflection — When Love Becomes Worship

When both people put God first, pride loses its voice. When both people lead with service, selfishness loses power.

Every act of humility in love mirrors Christ — who gave, forgave, and restored. Partnership becomes worship when you see your relationship as ministry, not maintenance.

Love is no longer about who's right; it's about who's willing.

Closing Thought — Together on Purpose

Two hearts in agreement are stronger than one walking in pride. Partnership isn't perfect balance — it's perfect willingness. It's knowing that when you fight for peace instead of position, you're already winning.

Love that lasts isn't about power. It's about purpose.

And when two people share the same purpose, no distance, doubt, or difficulty can destroy what they've built together.

Chapter

7

HANDLING CONFLICT
WITHOUT LOSING CONNECTION

"They didn't fight often, but when they did, it turned cold fast."

Conflict is inevitable. Disconnection is optional.

Love doesn't fall apart because of differences — it falls apart when pride gets louder than peace.

Every relationship faces moments when emotions flare and patience fades. But the goal of conflict isn't to win — it's to understand.

You can be right and still lose connection.

Or you can be humble and keep the relationship intact.

A good man doesn't avoid conflict; he learns to navigate it without losing respect.

Expanded Reflection — When Peace Matters More Than Pride

When tension rises, our natural instinct is to defend. We want to be heard, understood, and validated. But often, both people are fighting to be right instead of fighting to be close.

You can't lead in love while trying to dominate it. Peace isn't weakness — it's emotional strength under spiritual control.

When you can stay calm while emotions swirl, you're teaching her something powerful: that safety doesn't disappear when disagreement shows up.

That's how intimacy grows.

Not through perfection, but through the steady decision to protect the bond while discussing the problem.

Faith Insight — The Spiritual Side of Disagreement

"A gentle answer turns away wrath, but a harsh word stirs up anger." — Proverbs 15:1

God never told us to avoid conflict; He told us to handle it with gentleness. Gentleness isn't silence — it's strength filtered through self-control. It means you can still speak truth, but you do it in a way that builds rather than breaks.

When your tone stays steady, even when emotions spike, you're living out the Spirit's fruit — patience, kindness, and peace.

That's leadership through love.

Everyday Example — The Turning Point Argument

They were both tired. She was crying, he was frustrated, and the argument was circling the same mountain again. Finally, one of them said, "Let's not lose us over this." That single sentence became their reset phrase.

It reminded them that the relationship mattered more than the disagreement. That's what mature love does — it remembers the team even in tension.

Expanded Reflection — How to Stay on the Same Side

When conflict comes, remind yourself: She's not the enemy; the problem is. Approach it like teammates, not opponents. Slow your pace. Lower your tone. Watch your words.

Your calm is her cue that the relationship is still safe, even when you disagree. You can't always fix the issue immediately, but you can protect the connection while working through it. And that connection — that sense of "we're okay" — is what makes reconciliation possible.

Practical Framework — Conflict Recovery Steps

1. Pause before you speak. Give emotions a moment to cool.

2. Pray before you react. Ask for clarity, not control.

3. Identify the real issue. The topic might be small, but the emotion is big.

4. Choose timing wisely. Don't talk when either of you is tired or triggered.

5. Speak from "I," not "you." "I felt hurt" invites healing; "You always…" builds walls.

6. Listen for understanding. Don't just wait for your turn — absorb her words.

7. End with peace, not pride. Even if the topic isn't resolved, reconnect emotionally.

Checklist — Handling Conflict Constructively

- Pause before you speak.

- Stay on the issue, not her identity.

- Listen through emotion, not around it.

- Take accountability early; it disarms defensiveness.

- Repair quickly — time apart in anger can harden hearts.

- End with reassurance — "We'll get through this."

- Pray together if possible — it softens spirits instantly.

Faith Reflection — Turning Conflict into Connection

Conflict doesn't destroy love — ego does. When you learn to argue with empathy and communicate without condemnation, you transform conflict into intimacy.

Every resolved disagreement becomes proof that love is strong enough to survive truth.

That's when faith in the relationship deepens — not because everything's perfect, but because both people refused to quit.

That's what God does in us — He corrects without condemning, guides without guilt, and restores what pride would've ruined.

Closing Thought — Fighting to Stay Connected

Don't fight to be right. Fight to understand. You don't have to win every debate to win her heart.

When your goal becomes peace instead of points, you'll discover that even conflict can draw you closer — because love that listens through storms always comes out stronger than before.

Chapter

8

EVERYDAY HABITS THAT KEEP EMOTIONAL CONNECTION STRONG

"It's not the grand gestures that keep love alive. It's the little habits."

Passion may start love, but consistency sustains it. What makes relationships last isn't constant excitement — it's daily attention. The ordinary moments are where intimacy either grows or dies.

Love doesn't fade because two people stop caring; it fades because they stop noticing. Small neglects add up. So do small acts of kindness.

The same daily rhythm that once drew you close can drift apart if it's left unattended. Connection isn't a feeling to chase — it's a practice to keep.

Expanded Reflection — The Power of Daily Attention

Love is like a garden. It doesn't need to be dramatic — it just needs to be tended. When you water it with gratitude, trim it with patience, and expose it to light through honesty, it flourishes.

Neglect doesn't look like cruelty; it looks like distraction. You stop greeting her the same way. You stop listening with curiosity. You stop praying together. And slowly, what was once sacred becomes routine.

If you want to keep emotional connection strong, start treating every day like it still matters. Because it does.

Faith Insight — Habits of Love Reflect Habits of Faith

"Let all that you do be done in love." — 1 Corinthians 16:14

The same way faith grows through daily prayer and reflection, love grows through daily intention. Both require consistency, humility, and gratitude.

When you make love a discipline instead of a mood, it stops depending on circumstances. It becomes steady — the kind of love that can weather frustration, fatigue, and time.

Love isn't about feeling inspired; it's about choosing investment.

Everyday Example — The Habit of Small Gestures

He used to leave sticky notes on her coffee cup. When life got busy, he stopped — and she noticed. Weeks later, he started again. No big speech. Just a simple "Have a great day, beautiful." And she smiled the way she used to.

Love didn't need fireworks. It just needed consistency. Small gestures reignite big warmth.

Expanded Reflection — The Three Pillars of Daily Connection

1. Gratitude — Thank her for something real every day. Gratitude turns routine into reverence.

2. Presence — Show up, not just physically but emotionally. Even a five-minute check-in matters.

3. Prayer — Pray with her when you can, and for her when you can't. It keeps the bond anchored beyond words.

When you live these three pillars, you stop wondering if the spark will fade — you're too busy tending the flame.

Practical Framework — 7 Daily Connection Habits

1. Morning Intent — Set the tone with kindness before the day starts.

2. Daily Gratitude — Speak one thank-you out loud.

3. Midday Check-In — A short "How's your day?" without agenda.

4. Thoughtful Affection — A text, a touch, or a smile to say "I see you."

5. One Full Listen — Give her five undivided minutes.

6. Evening Peace — End the day in calm, not chaos.

7. Keep Humor Alive — Laughter heals what words can't.

These simple rhythms build a quiet, unshakable intimacy — the kind that feels like home.

Checklist — Keeping Emotional Connection Alive

- Don't assume — ask.
- Protect time together, even when busy.
- Affirm her worth frequently.
- Address distance early, before it grows.
- Keep gratitude and prayer at the center.
- Never stop learning her.
- Remember: consistency is romance.

Faith Reflection — When Routine Becomes Sacred

When love becomes routine, many people panic — they think it's fading. But routine isn't the enemy of passion; it's the container that protects it.

God works through habits. So does love. The rhythm you create together is the rhythm that will carry you through hard seasons. Your small daily acts become holy ground where peace and affection grow side by side.

Closing Thought — Love That Lasts Is Built, Not Found

Don't chase excitement — cultivate consistency. Don't search for magic — create meaning.

Remember her every day, in every way, and you'll never have to wonder if the spark is gone.

Love that is cared for daily doesn't fade — it deepens. And when it's rooted in faith, even time can't undo it.

Chapter

9

DISCERNMENT
AND MUTUAL EFFORT

———————————

"Love isn't proven by words. It's revealed by effort." Discernment is love's safeguard. It's what helps you tell the difference between a connection that needs patience and one that needs peace — between a season that's testing your faith and a situation that's draining your soul.

Good men love deeply — but sometimes deeply turns into depletion. That's why discernment matters.

You can be sincere, but sincerity without wisdom gets used.

Love without boundaries becomes exhaustion dressed as devotion.

Expanded Reflection — Seeing Love for What It Is

There's a difference between chasing peace and chasing people. One leads you closer to God; the other leaves you confused.

If you're always the one initiating, apologizing, explaining, or adjusting — stop and ask yourself, "Is this love, or is this labor?"

Healthy love feels like partnership, not performance. It doesn't make you feel small for caring deeply. It meets you in the middle — not because it has to, but because it wants to.

Discernment isn't about suspicion — it's about clarity. It's not accusing; it's assessing. It's not closing your heart; it's protecting it with prayer.

Faith Insight — Wisdom Over Emotion

"Do not be unequally yoked." — 2 Corinthians 6:14

That scripture isn't just about marriage — it's about alignment.

It's about walking beside someone whose faith, values, and vision move in the same direction.

When you're unequally yoked, love turns into tug-of-war. When you're equally yoked, love turns into teamwork.

Wisdom protects what emotion can't always see — because sometimes what feels like chemistry is really confusion dressed in connection.

Everyday Example — When He Finally Understood

He had been trying for months — texting first, planning visits, keeping conversations alive. Every time she pulled back, he tried harder. Every time she went silent, he reached out again.

Then one morning, during prayer, he heard this whisper in his heart: "You're loving her with energy that should be healing you."

That hit deep. He realized love isn't meant to be chased — it's meant to be cherished.

He didn't stop caring. He just stopped carrying it alone. He loved her enough to let her match him — or lose him. And that peace was louder than her silence.

Expanded Reflection — The Signs of Mutual Effort

Mutual effort doesn't mean perfect balance every day — it means shared intent. You both want it to work, and you both show it.

Signs of mutual effort:

- She communicates, not just responds.
- She checks in without being prompted.
- She matches your tone of peace, not pressure.
- She shows respect even in disagreement.
- She invests energy when things get hard.

When that effort is missing, no amount of chasing will create it. Love is a seed that only grows when both people water it.

Practical Framework — Practicing Discernment

1. Watch patterns, not promises. People can say anything — consistency tells the truth.

2. Pay attention to peace. If you feel constant anxiety or confusion, God may be showing you it's time to pause.

3. Notice reciprocity. Healthy love gives and receives. If it only flows one way, it's not a partnership.

4. Protect your emotional energy. Not everyone deserves access to your heart; wisdom decides who stays.

5. Seek counsel and pray. Ask God for clarity before you make conclusions; He reveals what people try to hide.

Prayer for Discernment and Balance

"Lord, give me wisdom beyond my emotions. Let me see love for what it truly is, not what I hope it to be. Help me recognize effort as the language of sincerity.

When I'm tempted to chase, remind me that real love meets me halfway.

Teach me to love without losing myself, and to wait for the one who loves with the same depth and devotion. In Jesus' name, Amen."

Closing Reflection

Discernment isn't cold; it's caring with boundaries. It's loving with your eyes open — not out of fear, but out of faith. A good man knows his worth, but a wise man guards it. Because the right woman won't drain his heart to prove her love; she'll protect his peace to prove hers.

Chapter

10

KEEPING LOVE VIBRANT

"Love doesn't stay alive by accident — it stays alive by attention."

Many couples don't fall out of love; they fall out of rhythm.

What once felt effortless becomes background noise. Work, stress, distance, and routine start taking center stage. But connection doesn't fade because the feeling disappears — it fades because the focus shifts.

Keeping love vibrant means stewarding affection the same way you steward faith — through daily renewal.

Love is like a fire: if you don't feed it, it doesn't burn out overnight — it cools slowly, quietly, almost politely. But a good man notices early and chooses to rekindle before the warmth is gone.

Expanded Reflection — The Discipline of Delight

Love that lasts is intentional. It requires curiosity after comfort, gratitude after familiarity, and humility after misunderstanding.

Keep asking questions about her world, even after years together. Keep noticing her laugh, her tone, her tired sighs. When you stop studying her, you start assuming her — and assumption is where intimacy goes to sleep.

Vibrant love doesn't happen because you never argue; it happens because you keep choosing awe even when you know the details.

Faith Insight — Love That Reflects God's Joy

"I have come that they may have life, and have it to the full." — John 10:10

Fullness isn't measured in possessions — it's measured in presence. A relationship built on faith should feel alive, not drained.

God didn't design love to feel like constant survival; He designed it to be renewal.

When you keep laughter, prayer, and gratitude in your rhythm, joy returns naturally. Faith brings fun back into love — not immaturity, but lightness.

Everyday Example — When They Started Laughing Again

They were together for years. Bills, schedules, and silent dinners had become their new normal.

One evening he turned on her favorite old song, the one they danced to before life got heavy. She smiled — that same smile from their first summer together — and for a moment, time bowed to memory.

He realized love never really leaves; it just waits for someone to make room for it again. That night, laughter came back — not because anything changed, but because they did.

Expanded Reflection — Four Ways to Keep Love Vibrant

1. Stay Curious. Keep learning each other. Ask questions no one else asks.

2. Keep Flirting. Light compliments cost nothing but build connection.

3. Create Moments. Plan simple memories — walks, prayers, small adventures.

4. Guard Your Tone. How you speak builds or breaks desire. Peace is attractive.

Vibrancy isn't found in novelty; it's found in renewed attention.

Practical Framework — Weekly Connection Check-In

1. What went well this week?

2. What felt off or distant?

3. What do we both need more of next week?

4. How did we pray together or for each other?

5. What's one small way to show love this weekend?

Five questions. Fifteen minutes. One habit that keeps hearts aligned.

Faith Reflection — Gratitude as Fuel

Gratitude keeps love alive longer than passion ever could.

When you thank God for your partner instead of comparing them, your focus shifts from lack to blessing. Gratitude changes the atmosphere — it reminds both hearts that the gift is greater than the grind.

Closing Reflection — Love That Keeps Growing

Vibrant love isn't loud — it's alive. It breathes through prayer, laughter, service, and gratitude.

When both people keep watering what they planted, love stops being fragile and starts being fruitful.

"The right love doesn't need to be chased — it needs to be cherished."

CONCLUSION

L ove is work, but it's holy work. It asks you to show up when you'd rather shut down, to forgive when it's easier to flee, and to believe again even after disappointment. Good men don't love perfectly — they love persistently.

Every chapter in this book has pointed toward one truth: connection is sustained by intention.

When you lead with humility, listen with empathy, and love with discernment, you become the kind of man who doesn't just keep love — he cultivates it.

This isn't the end of your story; it's the start of a stronger one. Take what you've learned, pray over it, and live it daily. Because the world still needs good men — men who love beyond the words.

FINAL DEDICATION

To every good man who's ever loved deeply, lost painfully, or prayed faithfully — may this remind you that your kindness is your strength, not your flaw.

Keep loving with purpose. Keep believing in grace. The world is better because you still care.

ABOUT THE AUTHOR

Logan Hart is the pen name of a lifelong believer in faith-driven love and emotional strength.

Drawing from personal experience and decades of observation, he writes for men who want to connect with women through authenticity, patience, and prayer.

His work through Logan Hart Publishing LLC seeks to restore the honor in good men — men who listen, lead with love, and refuse to believe that goodness is weakness.

When he's not writing, Logan enjoys technology and long conversations about life, faith, and purpose. He believes every man can learn to love better — starting with understanding.

COLOPHON

Beyond the Words: How Good Men Connect with Women

First Edition — November 2025

© 2025 Logan Hart Publishing LLC ISBN 979-8-218-84657-2

www.ingramcontent.com/pod-product-compliance
Lightning Source LLC
LaVergne TN
LVHW052038080426
835513LV00018B/2384